Ages 2 & 3
Undercover Heroes of the Bible

Rainbow Publishers

Rainbow Publishers · P.O. Box 261129 · San Diego, CA 92196

Ages 2&3

Undercover Heroes of the Bible

Angela Bowen Herrmann
Donna Bowen McKinney

Dedicated to our mothers-in-law, Tish Herrmann and Hallie McKinney. Thank you for your godly example and the wonderful sons you raised.

UNDERCOVER HEROES OF THE BIBLE/AGES 2&3
©2002 by Rainbow Publishers, second printing
ISBN 1-58411-009-0
Rainbow reorder# RB38071

Rainbow Publishers
P.O. Box 261129
San Diego, CA 92196

Illustrator: Chuck Galey
Editor: Christy Allen

Scriptures are from the *Holy Bible: New International Version* (North American Edition), ©1973, 1978, 1984 by the International Bible Society. Used by permission of Zondervan Bible Publishers.

Printed in the United States of America

Table of Contents

Memory Verse Index

Introduction

The familiar Bible stories with their familiar heroes are wonderful. We can learn a lot by telling those stories over and over again. But what about the less familiar people of the Bible? Most people can remember parts of the stories of Moses, Noah or John the Baptist. However, the Bible is full of people who are not quite so famous or familiar to us. These "unsung heroes" were still an exciting part of God's story. There is much to be learned from studying about them, too.

All of the activities in *Undercover Heroes of the Bible* were designed especially for two- and three-year-olds. The lessons are arranged in alphabetical order, but you can use them in any order you want. Once you select a lesson, the book guides you through the teaching and activity time.

The lessons are designed to be easy to use. There is a Bible story about each hero. Each story is followed by "Talk It Over" questions to help young students apply the Bible story to their lives, and a prayer for the class. Then there are two activities per story: crafts, games, puzzles or songs. Following the activities there is a "Note to Families" for each lesson. Duplicate these for each student, write his or her name on the top and include comments about the child or the day's lesson. Because toddlers often cannot recall specific lessons, families will appreciate these reminders of what their children learned so they can review the lessons with them at home.

Help the students learn to love these *Undercover Heroes* and grow closer to God.

Aaron • Family Helper

Memory Verse: If one falls down, his friend can help him up. (Ecclesiastes 4:10)

A Helpful Brother

Open your Bible to Exodus 4:10-17.

Then tell the Bible story:

Moses was in the desert taking care of the sheep when God called his name. God had a special job for Moses to do. He told Moses to go to Egypt and tell the ruler there to let God's people go free. God's people had been prisoners in Egypt for a long time.

Moses was afraid that he could not do this job. He made excuses and told God that he could not talk very well. God told Moses not to worry. God sent Aaron, Moses' brother, to help him.

Aaron was happy to see Moses. Aaron went with Moses to see the ruler of Egypt. God told them what to say to the ruler. Aaron said the words to the ruler. God also told Moses to take a special staff with him to Egypt. The staff was a wooden stick. God had Moses use the staff to perform great miracles.

Talk It Over

What things can you do to be a helper to your brothers, sisters or friends?

Pray

God, help us to be kind helpers like Aaron was to Moses. Amen.

Helping Hands Mural

What You Need

- white poster paper
- markers
- tape
- washable acrylic paint
- foil pie pans
- disposable hand wipes
- paint smocks

Before Class

Tape the white paper on the wall so that it is at the right height for children to make their hand prints. Using a marker, write "Helping Hands" on the mural. Use lettering like the example below so that the children will be able to make hand prints inside the lettering. Help the children into paint smocks to protect their clothing (men's old shirts work well).

What to Do

1. Pour paint in foil pie pans and place it in front of the mural.

2. Have the children place their hands in the pan, then make hand prints inside the "Helping Hands" lettering.

3. After they have completed the letters and they are filled in, wash the children's hands and remove their smocks.

4. Join together again in a circle in front of the mural. Talk about how the students all helped and worked together to make the mural. Remind them that everyone was important in making the mural. Say, **God wants us to be good helpers**.

5. Talk about ways that the students can be good helpers at home, church and with friends. Write their ideas randomly on the mural.

Aaron Picture Point

Aaron helped his brother Moses. Point to each picture below and talk about how the people in that family could help each other. Then color the pictures.

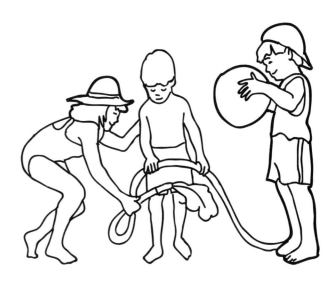

If one falls down, his friend can help him up.
Ecclesiastes 4:10

Dear Family of _____

In today's lesson, we talked about how Aaron helped his brother Moses. When God called Moses to do a special job, Moses was afraid that he could not do it. God told Moses not to worry. Then God sent Moses' brother Aaron to help him. God wanted Moses and Aaron to go together to tell the ruler of Egypt to let God's people go free. Moses and Aaron worked together to do the special job God had for them. Our memory verse is below. Please practice saying it with your child.

Comments: _____

_____

_____

If one falls down, his friend can help him up.
Ecclesiastes 4:10

- -

Memory Verse: I will obey your word. (Psalm 119:17)

A Shepherd Who Obeyed God

Open your Bible to Amos 7:14-15.

Then tell the Bible story:

Amos did not plan to be a preacher or teacher for God. Amos was just a man who took care of his sheep. We call him a shepherd. Amos also was a farmer who took care of sycamore-fig trees.

One day God called Amos to do a special job. God needed Amos to be a prophet – someone who preaches and tells people what God wants them to do. The people who lived around Amos had stopped obeying God. The people had a lot of money, but they disobeyed God. God told Amos to preach to the people and tell them that they needed to follow God's laws.

Amos obeyed God. Even though he was just a shepherd, Amos told the people that they must obey God.

Talk It Over

1. Before Amos was a prophet, what kinds of jobs did he do?
2. What things can we do to obey God's laws? (love each other, be kind to each other, be a helper, etc.)

Pray

Help us to obey You like Amos did. Amen.

Macaroni Sheep

What You Need

- sheep pattern below
- elbow macaroni
- scissors
- white spray paint
- glue
- markers

Before Class

Make a copy of the sheep pattern below, trace it onto white poster board and cut one out for each child. Spray the elbow macaroni with white paint and allow it to dry.

What to Do

1. Have the children draw in the sheep's eyes and mouth with markers.
2. Help the children glue the white macaroni to the sheep's body to create a "woolly" coat.
3. Say, **Our sheep remind us of Amos. Amos was a shepherd who obeyed God.**
4. Write the memory verse on the back of each sheep.

Amos' Paths

Use your finger to trace Amos' path so that he can find his sheep.

I will obey your word.
Psalm 119:17

Dear Family of _____

In today's lesson, we talked about Amos. He was a shepherd and a farmer. But God called Amos to be a prophet who preached to the people. Amos obeyed God. He told the people that they must start following God's laws again. God gives us His rules for living in a very special book called the Bible. We can read the Bible and obey God's laws. Our memory verse is below. Please practice saying it with your child.

Comments: _____

_____

_____

I will obey your word.
Psalm 119:17

Andrew • A Disciple

Memory Verse: Go and make disciples. (Matthew 28:19)

Telling His Brother the Good News

Open your Bible to John 1:35-42.

Then tell the Bible story:

People followed John the Baptist and listened to him teach. One day while John was teaching, he saw Jesus pass by. John pointed to Jesus and told the people that Jesus was the Lamb of God. John said this because he knew that Jesus was God's Son.

Two of the men who were listening to John left and went to talk to Jesus. They asked Jesus a lot of questions. Jesus spent the afternoon talking to the two men and answering their questions. One of the men was named Andrew. Andrew was a fisherman. He soon realized that Jesus was God's Son, also called the Messiah or Christ.

The first thing Andrew did was to go find his brother Simon Peter and tell him the Good News. Simon Peter was a fisherman like Andrew. Andrew brought Peter to Jesus so that he could meet Him. Both Andrew and Simon Peter became followers of Jesus.

Talk It Over

1. Can you tell your friends about Jesus?
2. What can you say to them?

Pray

Help us to be like Andrew and tell the Good News about Jesus to our friends. Amen.

Fishing Fun

What You Need

- fish patterns below and on page 19
- wooden stick or sturdy branch
- string
- magnet
- paper clips

Before Class

Make copies of the fish patterns so that every child will have three or four fish.

What to Do

1. Remind the children that Andrew was a fisherman when he met Jesus.

2. Give each child three or four fish. Have them color the fish and then help them cut out the fish.

3. Attach a paper clip to the mouth of each fish. Have the children help you put all the fish into a large bucket or basket.

4. Tie the string around the magnet. Tie the other end of the string to one end of the stick.

5. Let the children take turns trying to "catch" some of the fish. As they catch a fish, read aloud what it says on the fish.

Smile!
God loves you!

God
is good

Share
His Love

Jesus
loves me

Be kind
to one
another

19

Path to Church

Andrew met Jesus. Then he went home and told his brother Simon Peter about Jesus. Andrew brought Simon Peter to meet Jesus. This boy wants to bring his friends to church. Use your finger to trace the path he should take to find his friends and bring them to church.

Go and make disciples. Matthew 28:19

20

Dear Family of _____

In today's lesson, we talked about Andrew, who was a fisherman. Andrew met Jesus and talked to Him. Andrew was very excited when he realized that Jesus was God's Son. Andrew went home and found his brother Simon Peter, who was a fisherman, too. Andrew brought his brother to meet Jesus and both of them became His followers. Our memory verse is below. Please practice saying it with your child. Explain that Jesus wants us to tell the Good News about Him to other people.

Comments: _____

_____

_____

Go and make disciples.
Matthew 28:19

Memory Verse: I must preach the good news. (Luke 4:43)

Tent Makers and Teachers

Open your Bible to Acts 18:24-26.

Then tell the Bible story:

Aquila and Priscilla were married. They lived in a city called Ephesus. Together, they made tents and sold them to make a living. Aquila and Priscilla had heard the Good News about Jesus. But they did not keep this Good News a secret. They told other people about Jesus.

Sometimes Aquila and Priscilla invited people to their home and then told them about Jesus. They were not afraid to teach about Jesus to people they met.

Talk It Over

1. What kind of work did Aquila and Priscilla do?
2. What did they tell people who came to visit them?
3. Can you tell a friend about Jesus?

Pray

Help us to tell other people about God's love. Amen.

Aquila and Priscilla's Tents

What You Need

- tent connect-the-dots on page 24
- crayons or markers

Before Class

Make a copy of the tent connect-the-dots on page 24 for each child.

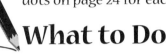

What to Do

1. Remind the children that Aquila and Priscilla made tents for a living.

2. Give each child a copy of the tent connect-the-dots.

3. Show the children how to use a crayon to connect the alphabet dots.

4. If the students need a little help, show them the alphabet letters printed at the bottom of the page.

5. Tell the students after they have connected the letter dots they can color the tent.

I Love Him So

What to Do

1. Remind the children that Aquila and Priscilla were faithful followers of Jesus and that they showed God's love to the people they met. Say, **We can be like Aquila and Priscilla.**

2. Teach the children the words to the simple song below, sung to the tune of "Three Blind Mice." Sing it together as a praise to God.

Love, Love, Love.
Joy, joy, joy.
Je-sus loves me so.
Je-sus loves me so.
He listens to me when I pray.
He listens to you when you pray.
I love Him, too.
I love Him, too.

ABCDEFGHIJKLMNOPQRSTUVWXYZ

Dear Family of _____

In today's lesson, we talked about Aquila and Priscilla, a husband and wife who lived in the city of Ephesus. Aquila and Priscilla worked together to make tents. They sold these tents to people who needed them. Aquila and Priscilla had heard the Good News about Jesus. They were excited to tell people they met about Him. Our memory verse is below. Please practice saying it aloud with your child.

Comments: _____

_____

_____

I must preach the good news.
Luke 4:43

Bezalel • Church Caretaker

Memory Verse: Come, let us bow down in worship. (Psalm 95:6)

Helping to Make God's House Beautiful

Open your Bible to Exodus 31:1-5.

Then tell the Bible story:

For many years the people traveled through the desert with Moses as their leader. They needed to have a place where they could worship God while they traveled. They could not build a church, like we have, because they were still traveling.

The church needed to be a tent that could be moved when they traveled from one place to another. This special tent for worship was called the tabernacle. This tent was big, with pretty decorations.

Many people worked to build the tabernacle. Bezalel was one of the workers. He was an artist who could make beautiful things out of gold, silver, bronze and wood. Bezalel used his talents to make pretty decorations for the temple.

Talk It Over

1. What are some of the things that you think are pretty in our church?
2. Isn't it good to have a church like this where we can come together to worship God?

Pray

Thank You, God, for our church and the people who come here. Amen.

26

Play Clay

What You Need

- 1 cup flour
- ½ cup salt
- 2 teaspoons cream of tartar
- 1 cup water
- 2 tablespoons oil
- pan
- aluminum foil
- zipper-style sandwich bags

Before Class

Mix the flour, salt, cream of tartar and water. Put the oil in a pan and heat it on a stove top. Add the mixed ingredients and stir. Cook for 3 minutes until a ball forms. Drop the ball onto foil and allow it to cool. Then knead it until it is a good consistency for playing. Store it in a zip-top storage bag to keep it fresh.

What to Do

1. Remind the children that Bezalel worked with his hands to make things for the tabernacle.

2. If possible, take the children on a brief tour of your sanctuary and point out the many pretty things there.

3. When you return to the classroom, give each child a small portion of play clay and let them make something they saw in the sanctuary. You may want to suggest things such as a Bible, tables, candles, pulpit, pews, etc.

Making Beautiful Things for Worship

God gave Bezalel the job of making the pretty things that would decorate the tabernacle — the place where the people went to worship God. Can you point to some of the things below and tell what they are? Then color them.

Come, let us bow down in worship.
Psalm 95:6

Dear Family of _____

In today's lesson, we talked about Bezalel, who was an artist. When the people of Israel were traveling through the desert with Moses, they did not have a church building where they could worship. But they did have a special tent, called the tabernacle, that could be moved when the people traveled. Bezalel had the special job of making beautiful things out of gold, silver, bronze and wood for the tabernacle. Bezalel used his special talent as an artist to help people worship God. Our memory verse is below. Please practice saying it with your child.

Comments: _____

_____

_____

Come, let us bow down in worship.
Psalm 95:6

Cyrus • A Good Friend

Memory Verse: There is a friend who sticks closer than a brother. (Proverbs 18:24)

A King Who Was Friend to the Jews

Open your Bible to Isaiah 44:28-45:6.

Then tell the Bible story:

Cyrus was the king of a country named Persia a long time before Jesus was born. Cyrus was a great leader. His army was very strong. Once he became king, Cyrus showed that he was a friend to the Jews.

The Jewish people, who worshiped God, had been held prisoner in a foreign land for many years. Cyrus and his army went to that land and set the Jewish people free. Cyrus wanted the Jews to be able to go back to their home in the city of Jerusalem.

Once they got home, the Jewish people were able to rebuild the temple and their houses. Cyrus showed what a good friend he was to the Jews by setting them free and sending them home. The Jewish people must have been very happy to be free.

Talk It Over

1. How can you be a good friend to other people?
2. How do friends treat each other?

Pray

Dear God, help us to always be kind to each other, like true friends. Amen.

Lace-Up Cards

What You Need

- poster board
- crayons
- yarn
- hole punch
- markers
- small magnets
- tape
- glue

Before Class

Cut the poster board into 4" x 4" squares, one per child. Write "Be Kind to One Another" on each square. Using the hole punch, make four holes along each edge of the square, spacing them about ¾" apart.

What to Do

1. Talk with the class about what it means to be kind to one another. Ask the children to name ways that they can be kind to each other and to their families.

2. Give each child a poster board square. Let the students decorate the square by drawing a picture of a way that they can be kind to someone.

3. When the students have finished decorating their squares, give them a piece of yarn. Tie a small knot on each end of the yarn. Help the children lace the yarn through the holes around the edge of the square (you might want to tape the sewing end of the yarn if the children are struggling).

4. Help the children glue the small magnet on the back of the poster board square.

5. Encourage the students to take home their magnets and put them on the refrigerator as a reminder to be kind.

Cyrus Picture Point

Cyrus was a friend to the Jewish people. How can you be kind to your friends? Point to the pictures below and talk about ways that you can show kindness to other people. Then color the pictures.

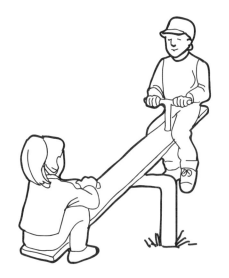

There is a friend who sticks
closer than a brother.
Proverbs 18:24

Dear Family of _____

In today's lesson, we talked about Cyrus, who was the king of Persia long before Jesus was born. Cyrus showed that he was a friend to the Jewish people, who worshiped God. For many years, the Jews had been prisoners in a foreign land. Cyrus led his strong army to that land and set the Jewish people free. Cyrus let the Jews go back to their homes in the city of Jerusalem. Our memory verse is below. Please practice saying it with your child. Talk about ways that we can be good friends to other people.

Comments: _____

_____

_____

There is a friend who sticks
closer than a brother.
Proverbs 18:24

Elisha • A Miracle Worker

Memory Verse: Elisha...prayed to the Lord. (2 Kings 4:32-33)

Healing a Sick Boy

Open your Bible to 2 Kings 4:8-37.

Then tell the Bible story:

Elisha was a man who told the people about God. God's power was with Elisha in a special way. Elisha could do things for God called miracles.

A man and woman who were friends of Elisha prayed that God would give them a baby. Elisha told them that God would answer their prayer and give them a baby.

Soon the man and woman had a baby boy. The boy grew, but one day he got very sick. Then he died. The man and woman were very sad. But right away, the mother traveled to where Elisha was staying and told him the bad news that their son had died. Elisha came home with the woman and prayed for the boy. God answered Elisha's prayer and a miracle happened. Suddenly the boy was well again. The boy sneezed seven times and then he opened his eyes. The woman was very happy that God had made her son well!

Talk It Over

1. Who was Elisha?
2. What did Elisha do when he heard that the boy had died?
3. Elisha showed that he cared for this family — how can we show that we care for each other?

Pray

Thank You, God, for caring for each of us. Amen.

Nature Walk

What You Need

- poster board
- tape
- markers

Before Class

Label the poster board "Things God Made."

What to Do

1. Remind the children that in today's story we heard about how Elisha cared about people. Say, **The Bible tells us that God cares for us and the world around us. Today we're going to take a walk and look for some of the wonderful things that God made.**

2. Take a walk outdoors with the children. Bring the poster board and tape along with you.

3. Point out the things that you notice in nature. Have the children stand still and listen for the sounds of nature.

4. If you notice nature things on the ground (leaves, nuts, twigs, etc.), have the children pick them up to display them on the poster board. Tape them to the poster board.

5. When the board is full, go back inside and talk about how God cares for all the things that He created in nature. Explain that it is important for us to take care of the world God has created for us.

Path to Elisha

The woman's son was very sick. She knew that Elisha could help. But first she had to go find Elisha. Use your finger to trace the road that she should travel to find Elisha.

Elisha...prayed to the Lord.
2 Kings 4:32-33

Dear Family of _____

In today's lesson, we talked about Elisha, who preached God's Word to the people who lived around him. God's power was with Elisha and he could do special things for God, called miracles. Today we talked about the miracle when Elisha prayed for a boy who had died. The boy's mother found Elisha and told him the sad news. Elisha prayed that God would make the boy well. God performed a miracle and the boy lived. Our memory verse is below. Please practice saying it with your child. Also, teach your child how to say a simple prayer, thanking God for family and friends.

Comments: _____

_____

_____

Elisha...prayed to the Lord.
2 Kings 4:32-33

Four Friends • Persistent Helpers

Memory Verse: A friend loves at all times. (Proverbs 17:17)

Helping a Friend in Need

Open your Bible to Mark 2:1-12.

Then tell the Bible story:

Four men had a friend who could not walk. He had been sick for many years. The four men heard that Jesus had come to their town. They knew if they carried their friend to Jesus that Jesus could do something to help him.

The four men laid their friend on a blanket. Then each of the four men picked up a corner of the blanket and carried their friend to Jesus. When they got to the house where Jesus was preaching, they saw that lots of other people had come to see Jesus, too. It was so crowded that they could not even walk into the room where Jesus was.

But the four friends had an idea. They decided to carry their friend up onto the roof of the house. In the time when Jesus lived, most of the roofs on houses were flat. Once the four men got their friend on the roof, they had to make a hole through the roof. They made a big hole in the roof and lowered their friend into the room to Jesus. Jesus healed the man and told him to get up and walk. The man who had not been able to walk for many years picked up his blanket and walked out. All the people who were watching were very surprised at what Jesus had done.

Talk It Over

1. What did the four friends do to help the man who could not walk?
2. What things can you do to help your friends?

Pray

Thank You for healing the man who could not walk. Thank You for the friends who helped him. Amen.

Four Friends Role Play

What You Need

- baby blanket
- baby doll

What to Do

1. Explain to the children that they are going to act out the Bible story of the four men who carried their sick friend to Jesus. Assign the following parts to the children: four friends, Jesus and the "crowd."

2. Arrange the chairs in a rectangle to resemble the outside of a house. In the middle of the "house," put four chairs with their backs to each other. Explain that instead of a sick person, the students will be using a baby doll to act out the story.

3. Retell the story in your own words. As you do, have the children act out the story. When you get to the part where the man is lowered through the roof, have the four friends lower the doll on the blanket to the floor in the area between the four chairs. Then move the chairs back and have the children act out the rest of the story as if they are in the room where Jesus healed the sick man.

Strong Arms Toss Game

What You Need

- bean bag or small, soft ball
- plastic bucket
- masking tape

What to Do

1. Remind the children that the four men brought their friend to Jesus because the friend could not walk. Say, **When Jesus healed the man, he stood up on strong legs and walked home. We should always thank God for our strong bodies.** Explain that the class is going to play a toss game using strong arms.

2. Place a piece of masking tape on the floor about five feet away from the bucket.

3. Have the children line up behind the tape line.

4. Give the ball or bean bag to the first person in line and ask them to try to toss it into the bucket. Cheer for everyone's attempt, whether it lands in the bucket or not.

5. Say, **We're so thankful for our strong bodies.**

Dear Family of _____

In today's lesson, we talked about four men who had a friend who could not walk. The four men loved their friend so much that they decided to bring him to Jesus because they believed that Jesus could help. Jesus healed the man. All the people who saw it were amazed. The four friends showed what it means to be a true friend. Our memory verse is below. Please practice saying it aloud with your child.

Comments: _____

_____

_____

A friend loves at all times.
Proverbs 17:17

Gideon • A Brave Man

Memory Verse: The Lord is with you, mighty warrior. (Judges 6:12)

A Soldier for God

Open your Bible to Judges 7:13-2.

Then tell the Bible story:

Gideon was a farmer. One day, God asked Gideon to do a special job. God wanted Gideon to lead the army to fight against soldiers from Midian, another country. Gideon did not think that he could do this hard job. But God promised to be with Gideon and to help him.

God gave Gideon a special plan for the army. Each soldier would carry a trumpet, an empty jar and a torch, which was a long stick with fire burning on one end. Gideon led the soldiers to the edge of the camp where the soldiers from Midian were sleeping. It was night time.

Then Gideon told his men to blow their trumpets, break their jars and shout, "A sword for the Lord and for Gideon." All the noise scared the army of Midian. Gideon and his soldiers easily won the battle. Gideon followed God's plan and his army won.

Talk It Over

1. Do you think Gideon was ever afraid?
2. Do you think it helped Gideon to feel brave when God promised to be with him?

Pray

Thank You, God, for being with us and taking care of us each day. Amen.

41

God Watches Over Me

What You Need

- paper plates
- paper fasteners
- scissors
- crayons

Before Class

For each child, draw a horizontal line and a vertical line on a plate so it is divided into quarters. Cut out a quarter section on each plate. Write on the plate, "God Watches Over Me." On the second plate, for each child, again draw two lines to divide it into quarters. Do not cut any sections out of this second plate.

What to Do

1. Remind the children that just as God watched over Gideon and his soldiers, He also watches over us. Explain that they will make a picture wheel to show the times that God is watching over them.
2. Give each child two plates and let them draw pictures on the plate that is not cut. Suggest that they draw a picture in each section, showing different times that God watches over them (for example, night time, when they are playing, at church, with friends, etc.)
3. When they finish drawing their pictures, attach the first plate with the cut out section on top of the plate with their pictures on it. Make a small hole in the center of both plates and insert the metal paper fastener. Let them turn the wheel and see how God watches over them all the time.

Gideon's Trumpets

What You Need

- trumpet pattern from page 43
- lightweight cardboard
- scissors
- aluminum foil

Before Class

Duplicate the trumpet pattern on page 43. Trace it onto cardboard and cut out one for each child.

What to Do

1. Remind the children how Gideon and his army won the battle, not with weapons, but with trumpets and jars.
2. Give each child a cardboard trumpet and a piece of aluminum foil. Help the students wrap foil tightly around the cardboard trumpet.
3. Briefly retell the Bible story, then lead the children in a march with their trumpets like Gideon's army.

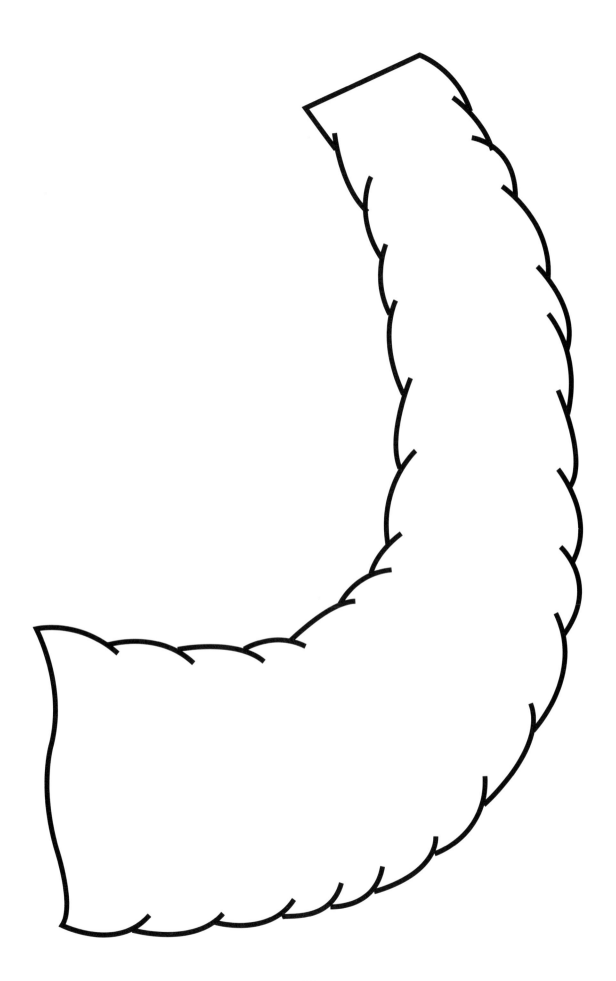

Dear Family of _____

In today's lesson, we talked about Gideon, who was a farmer. God called Gideon to lead an army in the fight against the Midianites. Gideon did not think he could do this hard job. But God promised to help Gideon. God gave Gideon a plan for the army. He said to carry a trumpet, an empty jar and a torch. Gideon did what God said. The army went to where the Midianites were sleeping. They blew the trumpets, broke the jars and shouted, "A sword for the Lord and for Gideon." The army was so confused and scared that they ran away. Just like He had promised, God helped Gideon win the battle. Our memory verse is below. Please practice saying it with your child.

Comments: _____

_____

_____

The Lord is with you, mighty warrior.
Judges 6:12

John • Jesus' Follower

Memory Verse: *"Come, follow me," Jesus said, "and I will make you fishers of men."* (Mark 1:17)

One of Jesus' Special Helpers

Open your Bible to Mark 1:16-20.

Then tell the Bible story:

When Jesus lived here on earth, He traveled from town to town, telling people about how much God loved them. Jesus had 12 special helpers who traveled with Him. These men were called "disciples."

John was one of Jesus' disciples. Before John met Jesus, he and his brother James were fishermen. They worked on a boat with their father, catching fish.

When Jesus met John, He asked John to be His disciple. He told him that he would now fish for men, which meant that he would help Jesus find more followers. Right away, John and his brother James left their fishing and began to follow Jesus.

John must have learned many things while he traveled with Jesus. He listened to Jesus teach and he watched Jesus help people. Later in his life, John wrote several of the books in our Bible.

Talk It Over

1. What was John doing before he met Jesus?
2. How can we follow Jesus like John?

Pray

Show us how to follow You. Amen.

Vegetable Painting

What You Need

- potatoes
- tempera paint
- paper
- small, shallow containers
- crayons
- paint smocks

Before Class

Cut the potatoes in half and use a small paring knife to cut out a relief design in the shape of a simple fish. If you want, you could also cut some other designs, such as a "J" for Jesus or a cross. Each child will need at least one half potato. Help each child into a paint smock to protect their clothing (men's old shirts work well). Pour the paint into the small containers.

What to Do

1. Remind the children that John was a fisherman. Explain that they will make a fish using a vegetable today.

2. Give each child a potato half and show how to dip it in the paint and then press it on the paper to make the fish design.

3. Allow the children to make more than one fish design on their paper, if they want.

4. After the fish have dried, have the students draw a picture of John catching the fish.

Outdoor Fun

Before John met Jesus, he was a fisherman who worked catching fish all day. Fishing is a fun thing to do. When we are outdoors, we can enjoy the world that God created. Can you draw a circle around some of the fun things that you like to do when you are outdoors?

"Come, follow me," Jesus said, "and I will make you fishers of men." Mark 1:17

Dear Family of _____

In today's lesson, we talked about John, who was one of Jesus' disciples. John and his brother James were fishermen before they met Jesus. Jesus called John to be a disciple. Jesus said that John would now be "fishing for men." John helped tell people about the Good News. Both John and James left their fishing boat and followed Jesus. Our memory verse is below. Please practice saying it with your child.

Comments: _____

_____

_____

"Come, follow me," Jesus said, "and I will make you fishers of men."
Mark 1:17

Joseph • Jesus' Earthly Father

A Good Husband

Open your Bible to Matthew 1:16-2:23.

Then tell the Bible story:

Joseph was a young man who loved a young woman named Mary. Joseph planned to get married to Mary.

Before they were married, Mary told Joseph that she was going to have a very special baby. This baby would be God's own Son, Jesus.

Joseph was very surprised. He knew that the people in his town probably would not understand what was happening to Mary. But an angel talked to Joseph about God's special plan and told Joseph that everything would be all right.

Joseph married Mary and took good care of her and baby Jesus when He was born. When Jesus grew up to be a boy, Joseph taught him how to build things with tools. Joseph obeyed what God asked him to do. Joseph was a good husband and a good father.

Talk It Over

1. Who was Joseph's wife?
2. Who was the special baby that Mary was going to have?
3. Who came to Joseph and told him about God's special plan for him and Mary?
4. Joseph obeyed God — what things can we do to obey God?

Pray

Help us to obey You all the time. Amen.

Touch and Guess Game

What You Need

- large paper bag
- straw
- small, plastic barn animal
- toy hammer
- small wrapped gift
- small baby doll
- Bible
- angel from a nativity set
- brown chenille wire

Before Class

Shape the brown chenille wire like a shepherd's staff. Place all of the items from the list above in the paper bag before the children arrive.

What to Do

1. Remind the children that the Bible story was about Joseph.

2. Explain that there are things in the bag that relate to parts of the story about Joseph and the Christmas story.

3. Tell the children that they cannot look in the bag, but that they will reach in the bag and feel the things there.

4. Give each child a turn to feel the items.

5. If they can correctly guess an item, let them pull it out of the bag.

6. Talk about how each item relates to the story (see below).

Straw: represents the manger where Jesus first rested when He was born

Plastic barn animal: represents that Jesus was born in a stable where the animals lived

Hammer: represents that Jesus learned from Joseph how to work with tools

Wrapped gift: represents the gifts that the wise men brought to Jesus

Baby doll: represents that Jesus came to this world as a baby

Bible: represents God's Word, where we can learn more about Him

Angel: represents the angels who brought the Good News of Jesus' birth

Shepherd's staff: represents the shepherds who came to see Jesus when He was born

Joseph the Carpenter

Joseph was a carpenter. He probably built chairs, tables and other things made of wood. A carpenter today uses many different kind of tools. Can you look at the tool pictures below and tell what each does? Then color the pictures.

Joseph...was a righteous man.
Matthew 1:19

Dear Family of _____

In today's lesson, we talked about Joseph, who was Mary's husband. God had a very special job for Joseph: he was to be part of Jesus' earthly family. The people in Joseph and Mary's town likely did not understand that Mary's baby would be God's Son. Joseph showed how much he loved Mary and baby Jesus by taking care of them. Our memory verse is below. Please practice saying it with your child.

Comments: _____

_____

_____

Joseph...was a righteous man.
Matthew 1:19

Joshua & Caleb • Trusted in God

Memory Verse: The Lord is good…He cares for those who trust in him. (Nahum 1:7)

Two Men Who Trusted God

Open your Bible to Numbers 13:1-31.

Then tell the Bible story:

Moses led the people of Israel on a long trip through the desert. They came to the edge of the land where God had promised the people they could build homes and live.

Before all of the people traveled into this new land, Moses sent a group of 12 men into the land. The 12 men looked around and saw what the land was like. They wanted to know if it would it be a good place for them to live.

When the 12 men came back to Moses, they had different stories to tell. Ten of the men told Moses that there were giants living in the land and that it would not be a good place for them to live. But two of the men — Joshua and Caleb — brought back a good report.

Joshua and Caleb said that they saw milk and honey and fruit in the land. Joshua and Caleb believed that the land was a good place to live. They knew that God would take care of them in the new land.

Talk It Over

1. How many men went to look at the new land?
2. How many men brought back a good report? Isn't it good that we can trust in God, just like Joshua and Caleb? God will take care of us.

Pray

Thank You for taking care of us everywhere we go. Amen.

Promised Land Snacks

 ## What You Need

- milk in pint-size cartons
- seedless grapes
- bread
- honey butter
- small plastic sandwich bags

 ## Before Class

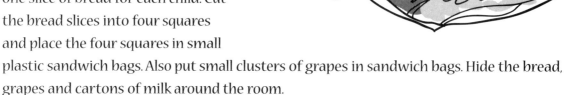

You will need one pint-size milk carton for every two children and one slice of bread for each child. Cut the bread slices into four squares and place the four squares in small plastic sandwich bags. Also put small clusters of grapes in sandwich bags. Hide the bread, grapes and cartons of milk around the room.

 ## What to Do

1. Remind the children that Joshua and Caleb looked around the new land to see what it was like.

2. Say, **They found that the land was flowing with milk and honey. Today we'll act like Joshua and Caleb and look for good foods that are hidden in our room.**

3. After the children have found the snack items, share them as a snack for everyone. Spread honey butter on bread slices for anyone who wants to taste it.

Good Food

Joshua and Caleb went to the Promised Land to see what was there. They found that the land was filled with good food for them to eat. Look at the food below. Draw a circle around the foods that are good for you to eat. Then color the pictures.

The Lord is good...
He cares for those who trust in him.
Nahum 1:7

Dear Family of _____

In today's lesson, we talked about Joshua and Caleb. Moses had led the people of Israel on a long trip through the desert. Before all of the people traveled into this new land, Moses sent a group of 12 men into the land. The 12 men looked around and saw what the land was like. When the 12 men came back to Moses, they had different stories to tell. Ten told Moses that there were giants living in the land and that it would not be a good place for them to live. But two of the men — Joshua and Caleb — brought back a good report. They knew that God would take care of them in the new land. Our memory verse is below. Please practice saying it with your child.

Comments: _____

_____

_____

The Lord is good...
He cares for those who trust in him.
Nahum 1:7

Josiah • A Believer in God's Word

A King Who Obeyed God

Open your Bible to 2 Kings 22:1-13 and 23:1-3.

Then tell the Bible story:

Josiah was just 8 years old when he became king. Josiah's father had been a very bad king who did not love God.

After Josiah was the king for 18 years, a very exciting thing happened. Men who were fixing the temple found a book of God's laws. The men brought the book to Josiah and read it to him. When he heard the words, Josiah knew that it was God's Word. Josiah knew that the people of his country had not been obeying God.

Josiah decided that it was time for a change. He asked God to forgive him for doing the wrong thing. Josiah led the people in obeying God. Josiah was a great king because he loved and obeyed God.

Talk It Over

Why is it good for us to read stories from God's Word, the Bible?

Pray

Thank You for the Bible, which shows us the ways to obey You. Amen.

Dear Family of _____

In today's lesson, we talked about Josiah. He became king when he was only 8 years old. Josiah's father had been a very bad king who did not love God. While Josiah was king, something exciting happened: men who were working on the temple found God's laws hidden in the trash. They brought the book to Josiah. When Josiah heard the words in the book, he knew that the people of his country had not been obeying God. He asked God to forgive them. Josiah was a great king! Our memory verse for today is below. Please practice saying it with your child.

Comments: _____

_____

_____

We will listen and obey.
Deuteronomy 5:27

Luke • A Servant

Memory Verse: Serve one another in love. (Galatians 5:13)

Dr. Luke

 Open your Bible to Acts 27:1-28:16.

Then tell the Bible story:

Luke was a doctor who loved God very much. In order to serve God, Luke traveled with Paul to share the Good News about Jesus with people everywhere. Traveling with Paul was not easy for Luke. Paul's ship wrecked, he was bitten by a snake and he was even thrown in jail while Luke was traveling with him. Because Luke was a doctor, he was probably able to take care of Paul when some of these bad things happened.

Besides being a doctor, Luke was also a writer. He wrote several parts of the Bible. Luke could have stayed in his home town and been a doctor who took care of the people there. Instead, he decided to serve God as a doctor by traveling with Paul. Luke was not afraid to use the special things that he had learned in order to serve God better.

 ## Talk It Over

1. What job did Luke do?
2. With whom did Luke travel?
3. How can you help your friends?

Pray

Thank You, God, that we are able to do so many things. Amen.

God Cares for You

What You Need

- bandage and label patterns from page 63
- glue
- crayons
- quart-size jar with lid

Before Class

Make a copy of the bandage and label patterns on page 63 for each child. Cut out the bandages and labels. Choose someone from the church or community who is ill or homebound.

What to Do

1. Remind the children that Luke was a doctor who cared for people when they were sick. Explain that the students will be making a medicine jar for someone who is ill. Tell about the person you have chosen to receive the jar.

2. Give each child a copy of the bandage pattern. Talk about how bandages are used and how they can help hurt people feel better.

3. Have the children decorate one side of the bandage with bright crayons. On the opposite side of the bandage, write statements, such as "God loves you," "Get well soon," "God cares for you," etc. (allow the children to select the statement from those you suggest).

4. When the students are finished with the bandages, let them fold them in half and place them in the jar. Tell the children that they have made these special messages to help the person who is sick to feel a little better.

5. Have the children decorate the small labels that say "God cares for you." Glue a couple of these labels on the outside of the jar. The labels that aren't glued on the jar can be taken home by the children and given to someone they know who is not feeling well.

6. Plan a time to deliver the jar to the person who is ill.

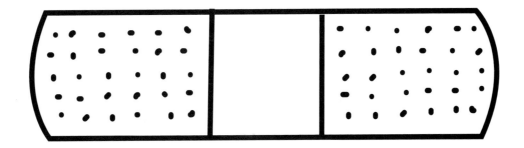

God
cares for
you

Toss and Talk

What You Need

- beanbag

What to Do

1. Have the children sit in a circle, either on the floor or in chairs.

2. Remind them that Luke showed love by the ways that he served God and helped Paul. Say, **Our memory verse today is "Serve one another in love." There are many ways we can show love to one another.**

3. Explain that you are going to toss the bean bag to someone in the circle. That person will name one way that people can show love to each other. Then that person will toss the bean bag to another person and the second person will name another way that we can show love to each other.

4. Continue in this way, tossing the bean bag and naming ways that we show love to each other until everyone has had a turn.

5. Encourage the children to practice showing love in everything they do.

Dear Family of _____

In today's lesson, we talked about Luke. Luke was a doctor who loved God very much. In order to serve Him, he traveled with Paul to share the Good News about Jesus with people everywhere. Because Luke was a doctor, he was able to take care of Paul when bad things happened. Luke wrote several parts of the Bible. Luke was not afraid to use the special things that he had learned in order to serve God better. Our memory verse is below. Please practice saying it with your child.

Comments: _____

_____

_____

Serve one another in love.
Galatians 5:13

Malachi • A Prophet

Memory Verse: God loves a cheerful giver. (2 Corinthians 9:7)

Gifts for God

 Open your Bible to Malachi 3:8-12.

Then tell the Bible story:

Malachi was a prophet — a person who preaches and tells people what God wants them to do. Malachi told the people that God was not pleased. The people were disobeying God's laws. The people were not bringing their offerings as a gift to God.

Malachi told the people that they were "robbing" God by keeping their offerings for themselves. God promised the people that He would take care of them in good ways if they would bring their offerings once again.

God gives us many blessings. We should always help the church and others by giving time and money.

Talk It Over

1. What are some good things you have? (for example, home, family, friends, etc.) Did you know that everything we have comes from God?
2. How can we thank God for all the good things He gives us?

Pray

Thank You, God, for all of the good things we have because of You. Amen.

Thankful Book

What You Need

- 3" x 5" index cards
- crayons
- metal rings
- hole punch

Before Class

You will need four or five index cards per child. Punch a hole in the upper left hand corner of each card. At the top of each card, write "I am thankful for." Group the cards together for each child and fasten a metal ring through the hole.

What to Do

1. Say, **Today's Bible lesson teaches us to be thankful for the things God gives us. We're going to make Thankful Books to remind us of things for which we can thank God.**

2. Give each child one of the Thankful Books. Let them decide what they would like to draw on each of their thankful cards. You may want to suggest some ideas like Jesus, friends, family, pets or nature.

3. When everyone has finished drawing, let the children tell the class about several of the things for which they are thankful .

Malachi Picture Point

Malachi reminded the people that all that they had came from God. The people had forgotten to thank God for all of the good things. Think about the good things you have. Everything we have comes from God. Can you point to the pictures below that show some of the good things that God gives us? Can you name other good things that God gives us? Then color the pictures.

God loves a cheerful giver.
2 Corinthians 9:7

Dear Family of _____

In today's lesson, we talked about the prophet Malachi. He preached to the people, telling them that they were "robbing" God because they were so greedy. The people disobeyed God's laws and would not bring their offerings to God. We bring our offerings to God because we love Him. Our memory verse is below. Please practice saying it aloud with your child.

Comments: _____

_____

_____

God loves a cheerful giver.
2 Corinthians 9:7

Mary & Martha • Learned to Listen

Memory Verse: Love the Lord your God with all your heart. (Matthew 22:37)

Two Sisters Who Loved Jesus

Open your Bible to Luke 10:38-42.

Then tell the Bible story:

Mary and Martha were two sisters who loved Jesus. They also had a brother named Lazarus. Sometimes when Jesus and His disciples were traveling, they stopped to visit in the town where Mary, Martha and Lazarus lived.

When Jesus came to visit, Mary loved to spend all her time sitting beside Jesus and listening to Him teach.

Martha was very busy when Jesus visited. Martha spent her time working in their home. She worked in the kitchen a lot, preparing food for everyone to eat. Sometimes Martha got angry because Mary was not helping her with the work. Jesus told Martha not to get so worried about who would do all the chores. Jesus wanted Martha and Mary to spend time with Him. He had many important things to tell them.

talk, talk! Talk It Over

1. What were the names of the two sisters who loved Jesus?
2. Is it sometimes difficult to listen when you would rather do something else?
3. How can we show that we love Jesus?

Pray

Help us to love You more each day. Amen.

Painted Cookies

What You Need

- three egg yolks
- one teaspoon of water
- one teaspoon of corn syrup
- food coloring
- refrigerated sugar cookie dough
- baking sheet
- rolling pin
- new, small paint brushes
- small paper cups
- assorted cookie cutters
- hand mixer
- milk or juice

What to Do

1. Remind the children that Martha liked to work in the home and probably enjoyed cooking. Explain that the class will be working like Martha by making cookies and then "painting" them.

2. Have the children help you roll out the cookie dough using the rolling pin.

3. Help the students cut out the dough using the cookie cutters. Place the cookies on the baking tray.

4. Use a hand mixer to beat the egg yolks, water and corn syrup. Divide this mixture into three small paper cups and add a few drops of food coloring to each cup. Give the children paint brushes.

5. Bake the cookies according to the package directions, but three minutes before they are done, remove the cookies from the oven and let the children "paint" them. Then return the cookies to the oven to finish baking.

6. After the cookies have cooled, serve them with milk or juice.

I Can Be a Helper

What to Do

1. Remind the children that Mary and Martha were sisters. Say, **God wants brothers and sisters to help each other when they can**.

2. Read the fill-ins aloud and have the children share an answer. If there are children in your class who do not have a brother or sister, mention that they can help their friends in these same ways.

When my brother cannot find his shoe, I can help him by _____.

When my sister asks me to share my snack, I can help by _____.

When my brother is picking up the toys, I can help by _____.

When my sister is feeling sad, I can help by _____.

Love the Lord

What to Do

1. Remind the children that the Bible memory verse is "Love the Lord with all your heart."

2. Teach the children the words to this simple song, sung to the tune of "London Bridge is Falling Down." Sing it together as a praise to God.

Love the Lord with all your heart
All your heart
All your heart
Love the Lord with all your heart
For He loves us so.

Trust the Lord with all your heart
All your heart
All your heart
Trust the Lord with all your heart
You can count on Him.

Dear Family of _____

In today's lesson, we talked about two sisters who loved Jesus. Mary and Martha were Jesus' friends. Sometimes Jesus visited their home. Mary loved to sit and listen to Jesus teach. Martha was usually busy when Jesus visited. She probably spent a lot of time fixing good food for Jesus to eat. Martha got angry that Mary wasn't helping with the chores. Jesus didn't want Mary and Martha to be upset with each other. He wanted the two sisters to listen to what He had to teach them. Today's memory verse is below. Please practice saying it with your child. Talk about ways to show we love Jesus.

Comments: _____

_____

_____

Love the Lord your God with all your heart.
Matthew 22:37

Mary Magdalene • First to See Jesus

Memory Verse: Jesus…appeared first to Mary Magdalene. (Mark 16:9)

The First One to See Jesus

Open your Bible to Mark 15:25-16:11.

Then tell the Bible story:

Mary Magdalene was one of the women who followed Jesus while He lived here on earth. Her first name was Mary and she was from a place called Magdala – that's why we know her as Mary Magdalene.

During the time that Jesus traveled from town to town teaching people, Mary Magdalene was part of the group of people who traveled with Him. When Jesus died on the cross, Mary was there watching. She stayed there at the cross, even when some of Jesus' other followers ran away because they were scared.

After Jesus was buried, Mary Magdalene came to the tomb where His body was placed. Mary was very surprised when a man dressed in white came and told her that Jesus had risen from the grave. This man in white was an angel. Mary was afraid because she didn't understand what had happened. Then Mary saw Jesus. Mary Magdalene was the first person to see Jesus after He arose from the grave.

Talk It Over

What happened to Mary Magdalene at the place where Jesus was buried?

Pray

Help us to be good followers of Jesus, too. Amen.

Bible Matching Game

What You Need

- Bible Matching Sheet below
- crayons
- scissors

Before Class

Make two copies of the Bible Matching Sheet below for each child.

What to Do

1. Have the children color the pictures that are in the squares of one of the Bible Matching Sheets. Point out that the pictures represent things in today's Bible story.

2. After they have finished coloring the items in the squares on their first page, help them cut out the squares on the second page. Cut out one set for yourself.

3. Mix up the squares, draw one at a time and show the square to the children. Let them find the correct match on their colored page. Once they find the match, have them put the picture on top of the matching square. Remind the children of how the pictures relate to today's story.

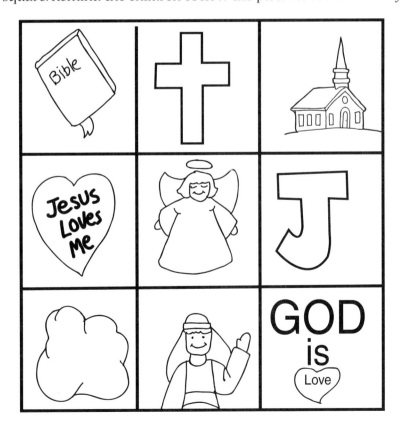

Mary Magdalene's Path

When Mary Magdalene found out that Jesus was alive and that He had risen from the grave, she told the Good News to other people. Use your finger to follow the paths that Mary should take to tell all of her friends the Good News. Can you tell your friends about Jesus?

Mary

Jesus…appeared first to Mary Magdalene.
Mark 16:9

Dear Family of _____

In today's lesson, we talked about Mary Magdalene. She traveled with Jesus, listening to His teachings. After Jesus died on the cross and His body was placed in a tomb, Mary came to the tomb. She saw an angel. Mary must have been surprised and afraid! But then Mary saw that Jesus was alive and standing in front of her. Mary Magdalene was the first person to see Jesus after He rose from the grave. Our memory verse is below. Please practice saying it with your child.

Comments: _____

_____

_____

Jesus…appeared first to Mary Magdalene.
Mark 16:9

Micah • A Believer

Telling About Jesus' Birth

 Open your Bible to Micah 5:2.

Then tell the Bible story:

Micah was a prophet — a person who preaches and tells others what God wants them to do. Micah lived about 700 years before Jesus was born. Many of the people who lived around Micah disobeyed God. Micah told the people that what they were doing was wrong. God wanted the people to stop doing wrong things and live His way.

Even though Micah lived a long time before Jesus was born, God let Micah know that someday God's Son would come to live on earth. Micah told the people that he knew that God's Son would be born in a town called Bethlehem. When Jesus was born, it was in Bethlehem, just like God had promised.

 ## Talk It Over

What parts of the Christmas story can you remember?

Pray

Thank You for Jesus and how much He loves us. Amen.

Finger Puppets

What You Need

- children's old knit gloves
- fine-tip permanent marker
- glue
- yarn
- fabric scraps

Before Class

Cut the fingers off of the gloves, one finger per student. Mark the eyes and mouth on each glove "finger" using the permanent marker.

What to Do

1. Explain that the students can choose one of the people in the Christmas story to make for their finger puppet.

2. Give each child one of the finger puppets to decorate.

3. Show how to decorate the puppet with yarn "hair" and clothes using the fabric scraps. They may use glue to secure the hair and the clothes.

4. Tie a piece of yarn around the body of each puppet to look like a sash.

5. Guide the children in acting out the Christmas story with their puppets.

Mary and Joseph's Path

Micah, the prophet, knew that Jesus would be born in the town of Bethlehem. Mary and Joseph traveled to Bethlehem just in time for Jesus to be born. Use your finger or a crayon to trace the road that Mary and Joseph must take to get to the town of Bethlehem.

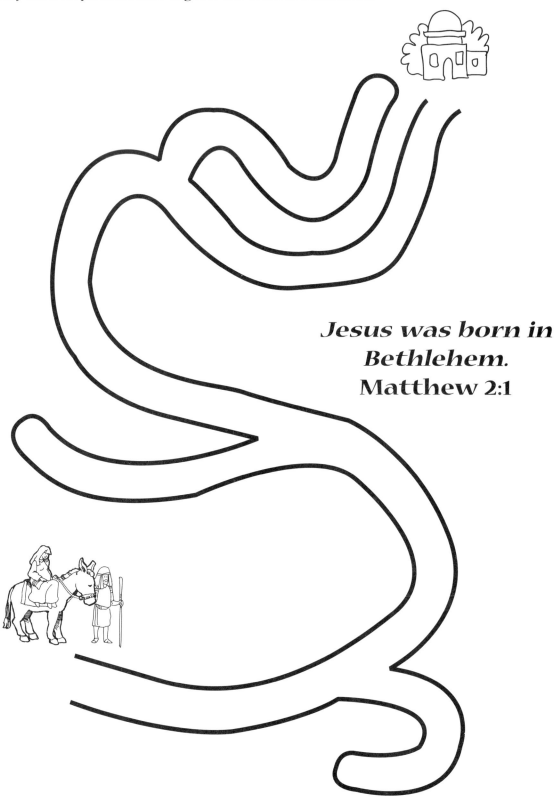

Jesus was born in Bethlehem.
Matthew 2:1

Dear Family of _____

In today's lesson, we talked about Micah, a prophet who lived many years before Jesus was born. Micah told people who lived around him that they needed to obey God. Micah also had a very special message for the people. God had told Micah that He would be sending His Son to live on the earth. He told Micah that His Son would be born in Bethlehem. God keeps His promises — hundreds of years later, Jesus was born in a town called Bethlehem. Our memory verse is below. Please practice saying it with your child. Retell the Christmas story about Jesus' birth in a stable.

Comments: _____

_____

_____

Jesus was born in Bethlehem.
Matthew 2:1

Nehemiah • A Hard Worker

Memory Verse: Come, let us rebuild the wall of Jerusalem. (Nehemiah 2:17)

The Wall Builder

Open your Bible to Nehemiah 2:11-18.

Then tell the Bible story:

Nehemiah was a prophet — a person who preaches and tells people what God wants them to do. Nehemiah and the Jewish people lived in a foreign country for many years.

Nehemiah knew that the walls of Jerusalem, his home city, had been broken down. It made Nehemiah very sad that the city walls were torn down. Nehemiah believed that God was leading him to fix the walls.

Nehemiah asked the king for permission to go home and fix the city walls. The king gave permission, so Nehemiah and the people went to Jerusalem. They worked together to fix the city walls. In only 52 days, the walls were finished.

Talk It Over

1. Do you think it was hard work to build the city wall?
2. How can we help each other with the jobs we do?

Pray

Thank You, God, for giving us strong bodies so that we can help each other. Amen.

Building Walls

What You Need

- building blocks

What to Do

1. Arrange the children into groups of two or three.

2. Give each group some blocks. Remind them that in the lesson Nehemiah helped to build the wall around the city.

3. Instruct each group to work together to build a wall.

4. When the walls are complete, have the students carefully tear it down, block by block.

5. Remind the students how sad Nehemiah was to see the walls of his city torn down.

6. Ask the children to work together to rebuild their walls. Say, **God wants us to work together and help each other in the jobs we do**.

People Who Help

When the broken down walls of the city needed to be fixed, Nehemiah and the people worked together. There are people who work to help us. Can you point to the pictures below and tell how these people help us? Then color the pictures.

Come, let us rebuild the wall of Jerusalem.
Nehemiah 2:17

Dear Family of _____

In today's lesson, we talked about Nehemiah, a prophet who preached God's Word to the people. For many years, Nehemiah and the Jewish people had been living in a city far from their homes in Jerusalem. Nehemiah knew that the city walls in Jerusalem had been torn down. This made Nehemiah sad. He knew that God wanted the walls repaired. Nehemiah went to the king and asked if he and the Jewish people could go home to repair the walls. The king agreed. The Jewish people worked together to repair the walls. Our memory verse is below. Please practice saying it with your child.

Comments: _____

_____

_____

Come, let us rebuild the wall of Jerusalem.
Nehemiah 2:17

Samuel • A Young Servant

Memory Verse: The Lord was with Samuel as he grew up. (1 Samuel 3:19)

Following God's Plan from the Start

Open your Bible to 1 Samuel 1:20-28 and 3:1-21.

Then tell the Bible story:

For a long time before Samuel was born, his mother prayed that God would give her a child. She was afraid that she might never have a baby. But God answered her prayers and Samuel was born.

Samuel's mother promised God that Samuel would serve God for all of his life. When Samuel was still a boy, his parents took him to live at the temple so he could be a helper there.

When he was living and working in the temple, Samuel heard God speak to him. God told Samuel that He had a special job for Samuel to do. As he grew to be a man, Samuel preached God's Word to all the people. God took care of Samuel as he grew up. But from the time he was a young boy, Samuel loved God and served Him.

Talk It Over

1. Where did Samuel live?
2. What did God say to Samuel while he was living in the temple?
3. How can we serve God now?

Pray

Thank You, God, for Samuel, who served You even when he was a young boy. Amen.

God Loves Me Place Mats

What You Need

- construction paper
- tempera paint
- clear, self-stick plastic
- aluminum pie pans
- disposable hand wipes
- markers

God
Loves
Megan

The Lord was with
Samuel as he grew up
1 Samuel 3:19

What to Do

1. Remind the children that Samuel loved
   God from the time he was a young boy. He loved God even more as he grew to be a man.

2. Give each child a piece of construction paper.

3. Pour a small amount of paint into an aluminum pie pan.

4. Show how to dip the palms of the children's hands into the paint. Let the excess drip off and then make two hand prints on construction paper.

5. Help them clean off their hands.

6. Allow the paint to dry partially. Then use the markers to write "God loves _____" (print each child's name in place of the blank) and the memory verse on the paper.

7. Point out to the children that each of the hand prints is different because God made each one of us different. Remind the children that God loves each and every one of us.

8. When the paint is completely dry, cover both sides of the construction paper with clear, self-stick plastic and trim the edges.

9. Encourage the children to use their place mats at home and compare their hand prints from time to time to see how they are growing.

Go to Church

When Samuel was a young boy, his parents took him to the temple. This family wants to go to church. Use your finger to trace the road they need to take to get to church.

The Lord was with Samuel as he grew up.
1 Samuel 3:19

Dear Family of _____

In today's lesson, we talked about Samuel. Before Samuel was born, his mother prayed that she would have a baby. God answered her prayers and Samuel was born. Samuel's mother had promised God that Samuel would serve Him. So while he was still a little boy, his mother took him to the temple so that he could be a helper there. Samuel grew to be a man who preached the Good News about God. Samuel loved God all of his life. Our memory verse is below. Please practice saying it with your child. Talk about ways to learn more about God.

Comments: _____

_____

_____

The Lord was with Samuel as he grew up.
1 Samuel 3:19

Silas • A Good Example

Memory Verse: Is anyone happy? Let him sing songs of praise. (James 5:13)

Singing Songs of Praise

Open your Bible to Acts 16:19-31.

Then tell the Bible story:

Silas loved God and was a good worker in His church. Sometimes he traveled with a man named Paul. Together, the two of them preached and told people they met about Jesus.

In one city, some of the people got mad because Silas and Paul were preaching. They had Silas and Paul put in jail.

Even this bad thing did not make Silas and Paul forget about how much they loved Jesus. While they were in jail, they kept on praying and singing songs about God. The other people in the jail wanted to know more about Jesus because Silas and Paul were good examples.

Talk It Over

It probably was hard for Silas and Paul to be in jail, but they still did not get sad. They were good examples. They kept on singing songs about Jesus. Do you have a favorite song about Jesus that you like to sing?

Pray

Thank You that we can be good examples by singing songs that praise You. Amen.

Praise Instruments

 ## What You Need

- small, empty containers with lids
- dried beans
- tape
- construction paper
- scissors
- glue
- Bible or music stickers

Before Class

You will need one container per child, such as a 20 oz. soda bottle or a yogurt container. Cut a piece of construction paper that will cover each container.

 ## What to Do

1. Remind the children that Silas and Paul sang praises to God even while they were in jail. Explain that the students will be making praise instruments to use when they are singing.

2. Give each child a container and a small handful of dried beans. Remind the students not to put the beans in their mouths.

3. Show how to put the beans in the container and then help the students secure the lid. If it is a snap-on lid, like a yogurt container, tape the lid to make sure it remains securely closed.

4. Help the children glue the construction paper around the container.

5. Write the memory verse on the outside of each container.

6. When the glue is dry, have them decorate the container with stickers.

7. Ask the children to name some of their favorite songs. Lead the children in singing the songs. Encourage them to play their instrument while they sing.

Music Picture Point

While Silas and Paul were in jail, they praised God by singing songs. We can praise God with our songs, too. We can also make music and praise God with musical instruments. Can you point to each instrument below and say its name? Have you ever seen a person playing one of these instruments? Color the pictures.

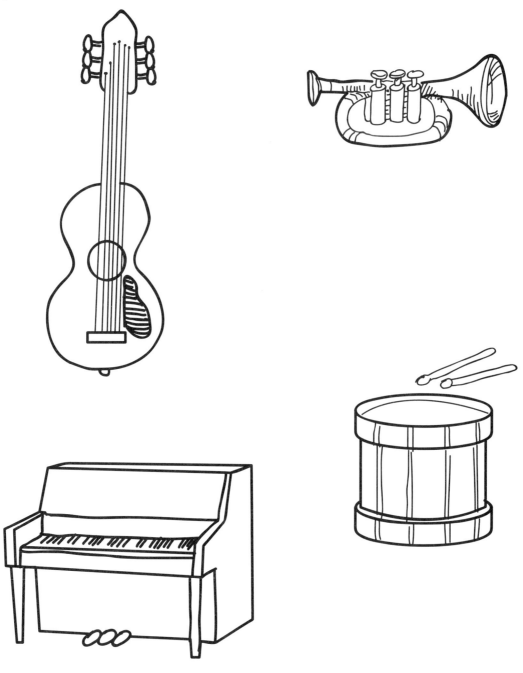

Is anyone happy? Let him sing songs of praise.
James 5:13

Dear Family of _____

In today's lesson, we talked about Silas and Paul, who were put in jail for telling the Good News about Jesus. Even in jail, they did not stop talking about Him. They sang songs of praise to God. When the jailer heard them, he wanted to know more about Jesus. Silas and Paul told the jailer about Jesus. Because of this, the jailer believed in Jesus, too. Our memory verse is below. Please practice saying it aloud with your child. Sing songs about Jesus in your home during the week.

Comments: _____

_____

_____

Is anyone happy? Let him sing songs of praise.
James 5:13

Memory Verse: The time came for the baby to be born. (Luke 2:6)

Celebrating Jesus' Birth

Open your Bible to Isaiah 2:22-38.

Then tell the Bible story:

Simeon and Anna loved God very much. They went to the temple each day to pray. Simeon and Anna were both getting old. They were hoping to get to see the birth of God's Son before they died. God had promised Simeon that he would not die until he saw Jesus.

One day Mary and Joseph brought Jesus to the temple. Jesus was still very young. As soon as Simeon saw Jesus, he knew that Jesus was God's Son. Both Simeon and Anna praised God because they had lived to see Jesus. They held Jesus and loved Him. They were so glad that the Savior had been born!

talk, talk! Talk It Over

What do we celebrate at Christmas time? (Jesus is God's gift to us.)

Pray

Thank You, God, for sending Jesus to be our Savior. Amen.

Star of David Ornament

What You Need

- craft sticks
- glue
- gold glitter
- ¼" red or green ribbon

Before Class

You will need six craft sticks per child. Cut a piece of ribbon for each child, about 6" long.

What to Do

1. Explain that the students will make a Star of David ornament for their Christmas trees to remind them of God's gift to us.

2. Give each child six craft sticks.

3. Help the children arrange three craft sticks in the shape of a triangle, with the ends of the sticks overlapping to form the three points. Glue the sticks together at the three points and allow to dry.

4. Help the children form a second triangle with the other three sticks. Glue the three points together.

5. Show how to place the second triangle on top of the first triangle, to form a star with six points. Glue the two triangles together at the points where they touch. Allow to dry.

6. Help the children put glue on the star and sprinkle gold glitter over it. Shake off the excess glitter.

7. When the glue and glitter have dried, tie the ribbon to the star in a loop to use in hanging the ornament.

Dear Family of _____

In today's lesson, we talked about Simeon and Anna. This man and woman loved God very much. Every day, they went to the temple to pray. Simeon and Anna were old, but God had promised them that they would live long enough to see Jesus. While Jesus was still very young, Mary and Joseph brought Him to the temple. When Simeon saw Jesus, he knew that this was God's Son. God had kept His promise to Simeon. Both Simeon and Anna praised God for letting them see Jesus in the temple. Our memory verse is below. Please practice saying it with your child.

Comments: _____

_____

_____

The time came for the baby to be born.
Luke 2:6